Learn to Carve a

WITCH

Pattern drawing by John Allard.

ISBN 978-1-56523-582-3 (kit)

ISBN 978-1-56523-625-7 (booklet only)

To learn more about the other great books from Fox Chapel Publishing, or to find a retailer near you, call toll-free 800-457-9112 or visit us at ***www.FoxChapelPublishing.com.***

Note to Authors: We are always looking for talented authors to write new books in our area of woodworking, design, and related crafts. Please send a brief letter describing your idea to Acquisition Editor, 903 Square Street, Mount Joy, PA 17552.

Second Printing
Printed in China

Learn to Carve a

WITCH

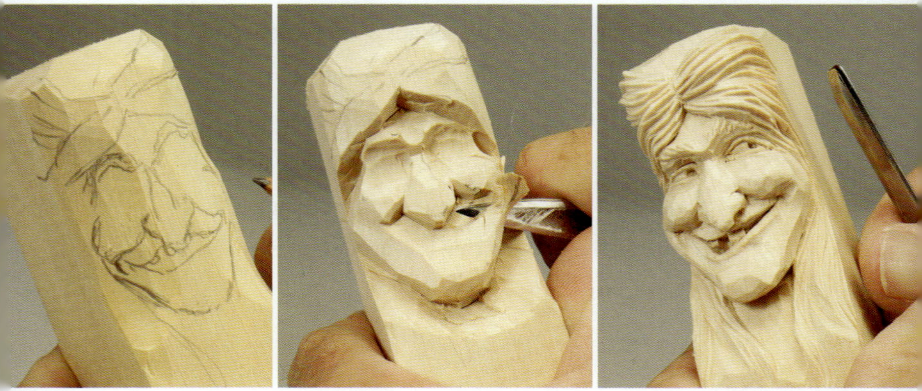

HAROLD ENLOW

FOX CHAPEL
PUBLISHING

Learn to Carve a Witch

While I call this a witch, it could easily be any sort of old ugly woman. You can give her a few more teeth and turn her into an old pioneer woman. Or add a beard or mustache and transform her into a circus performer.

Most of this carving depends on understanding how gravity and age affect the face. The hooked nose is a result of gravity pulling down and stretching the cartridge on the tip of the nose. The thin lips are caused by a loss of collagen and other plumping tissue in the lips. The pointed chin is caused by gravity and collagen loss.

I have listed what tools I use for this carving, but you can use whatever tools you have on hand—there is no need to use the exact tools I mention as long as you are pleased with the end result.

Prepare the blank. Round the corners of the blank. Sketch the major landmarks, such as the eyebrows, nose, lips, and chin onto the blank.

Carve the saddle of the nose. Carve down from the brow line and up from the middle of the nose to carve the saddle of the nose. Use a carving knife.

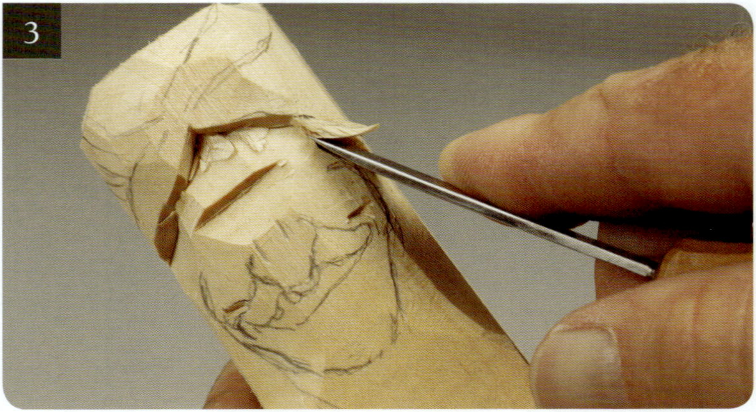

Separate the forehead from the hair. Taper the forehead from the top of the brow line to the hair line. Use a ⅜" #3 gouge. Stop-cut along the hairline. Then separate the sides of the face from the hair using the same tool. Deepen the cut at the saddle of the nose using a carving knife.

Separate the nose from the lips. Use a carving knife to make a stop cut at the bottom of the nose and cut up to the stop cut to separate the nose from the lips.

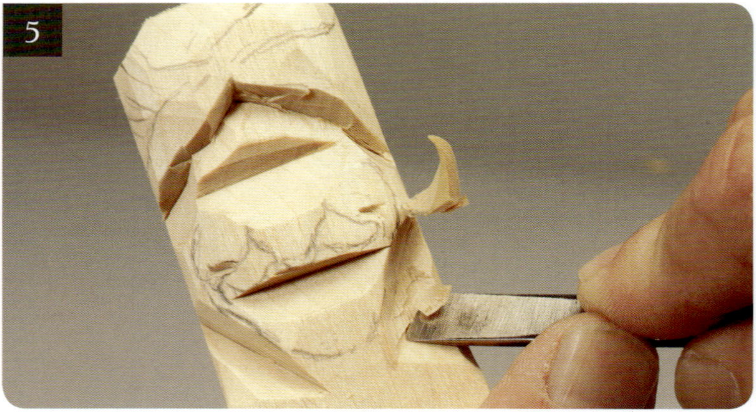

Separate the face from the background. Stop-cut along the face line with a carving knife. Carve up to the stop cut with a knife and a ⅜" #3 gouge to separate the face from the background.

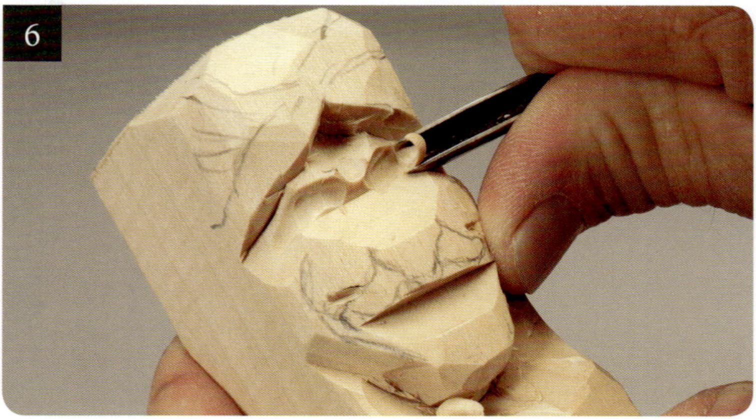

Carve the eye sockets. Use a ¼" veiner to deepen the eye sockets. Then use the same tool to separate the eyebrows.

Rough in the nose. Stop-cut alongside the nose with a carving knife or a ⅜" #3 gouge. Cut up to the stop cut to separate the nose from the cheeks.

Rough in the sides of the face. Carve up alongside the face to the hair line with a ⅜" #3 gouge. Cut along the hair line to separate the hair from the sides of the face with the same tool.

Separate the nose from the cheeks. Stop-cut alongside the nose and carve away the wood on the cheeks with a ⅜" #3 gouge. Shape the sides of the nose with a ¼" veiner.

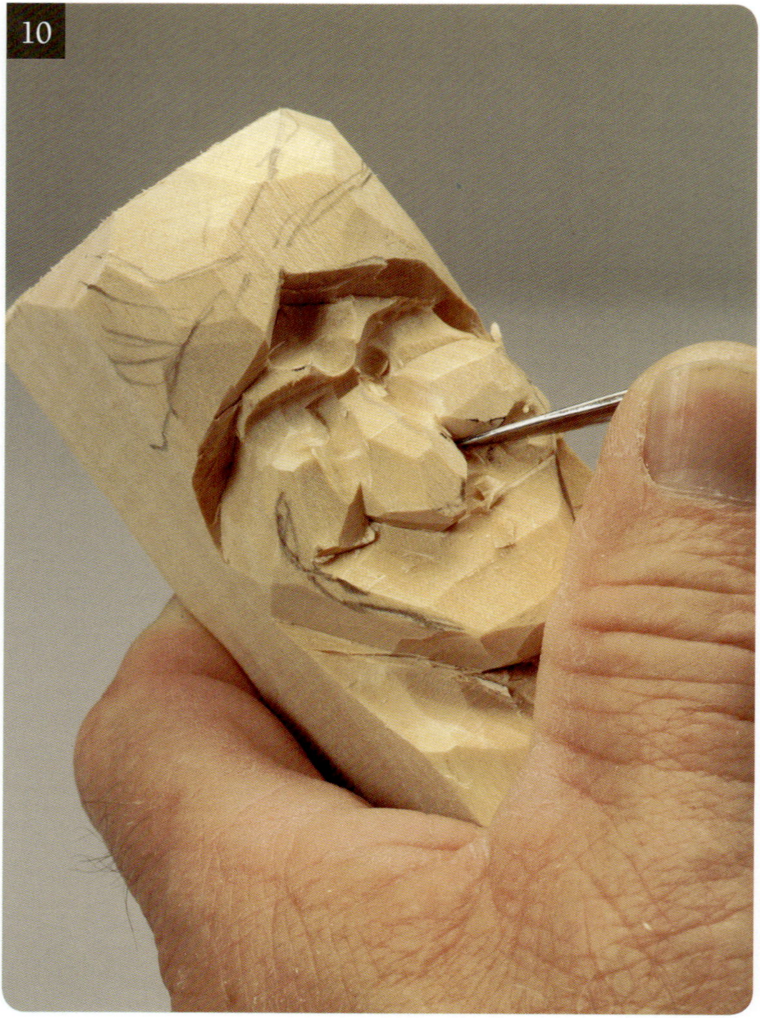

Shape the wings of the nose. Use a carving knife and a ⅜" #3 gouge to shape the wings of the nose.

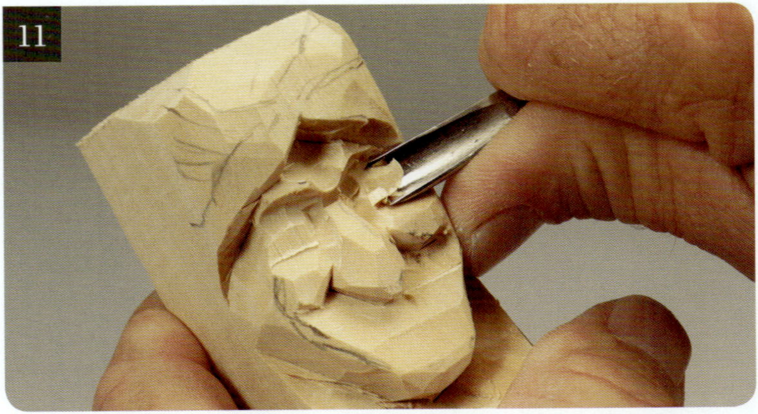

Deepen the eye sockets. Use a ⅜" #9 gouge to deepen the eye sockets. Round the top of the cheeks down into the eye sockets using a ⅜" #3 gouge upside down.

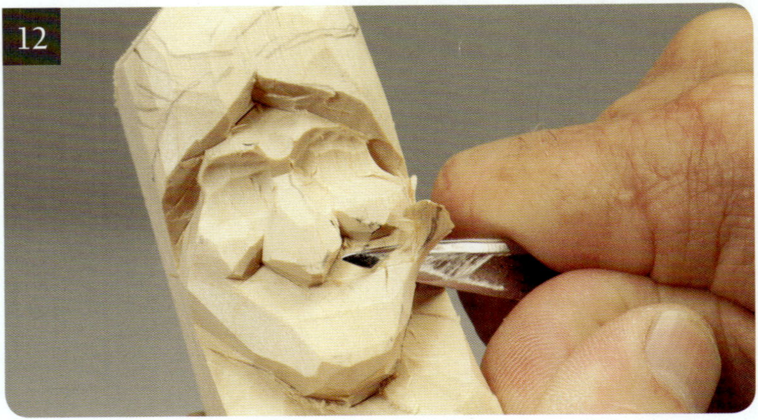

Thin the jowls. Carve along the sides of the face with a carving knife to create the thin pointed chin.

Finish roughing in the sides of the face. Carve the temple area and the end of the eye sockets using a carving knife.

Add the hook to the tip of the nose. Use the carving knife to undercut the tip of the nose to create a hook shape.

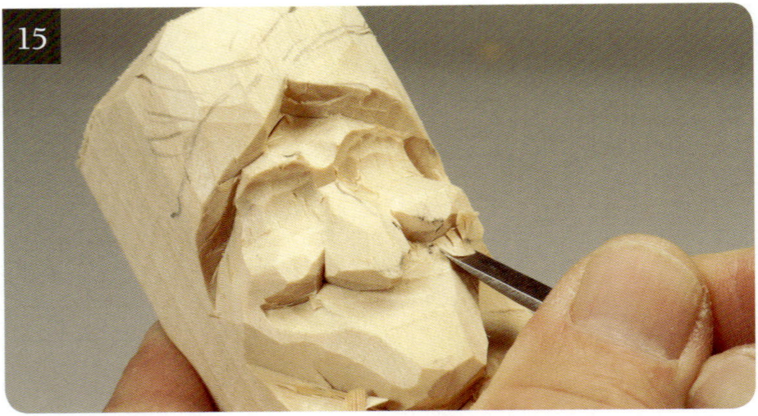

Accent the cheeks. Remove more wood from the area under the cheeks with a ⅜" #3 gouge to make the cheeks stick out more. The larger the cheeks, the more smiley the face looks.

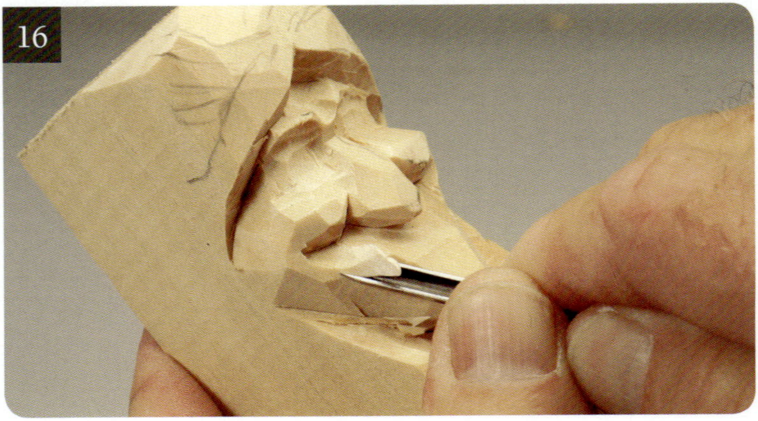

Thin the cheek and chin area. Use a ¼" veiner to carve grooves up alongside the face to the outside corners of the cheeks. This makes the face look like that of a thin old woman.

Deepen the area for the mouth. The pointed chin sticks out further than the mouth, so remove some wood in the mouth area with a ⅜" #3 gouge.

Rough in the mouth. Cut under the bottom lip with a small veiner to separate the bottom lip from the area under the lip. Stop-cut along the mouth lines with a carving knife.

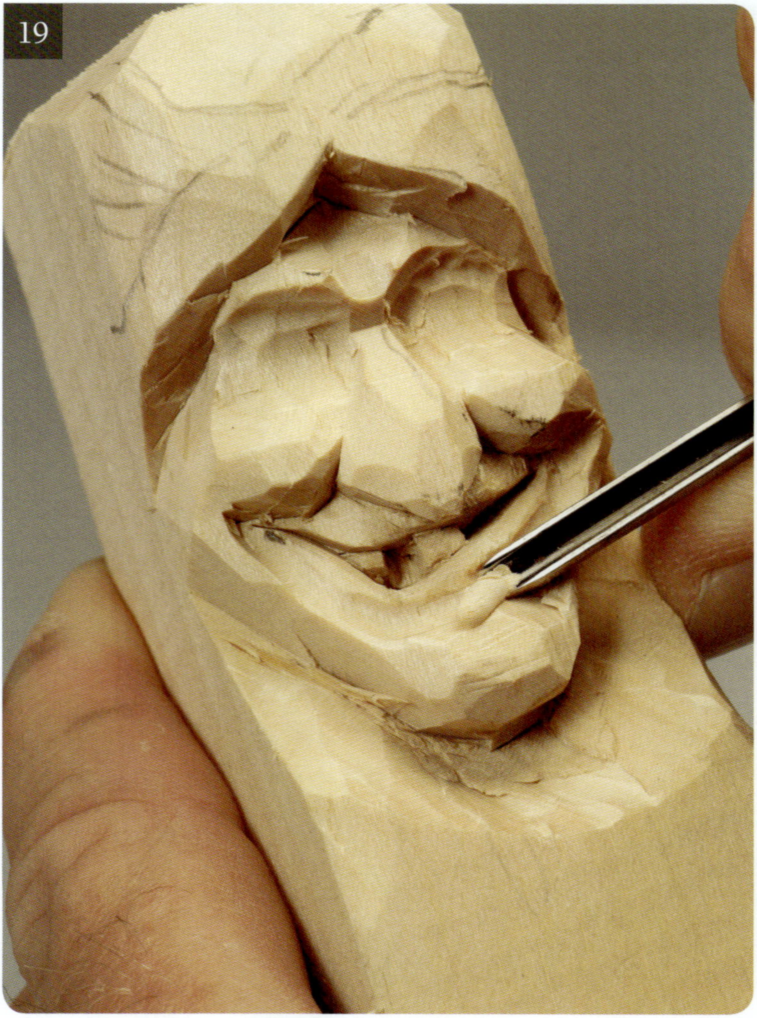

Finish shaping the mouth. Remove a bit of wood from inside the mouth to separate the mouth from the lips. Use a carving knife and a micro gouge to carve out the wood between the two teeth. Deepen the groove under the bottom lip, but make sure the bottom lip stays thin.

Shape the wings of the nose. Use a carving knife to remove a small wedge of wood from the sides of the nose to shape the wings of the nose. Carefully shape the bridge of the nose with a carving knife.

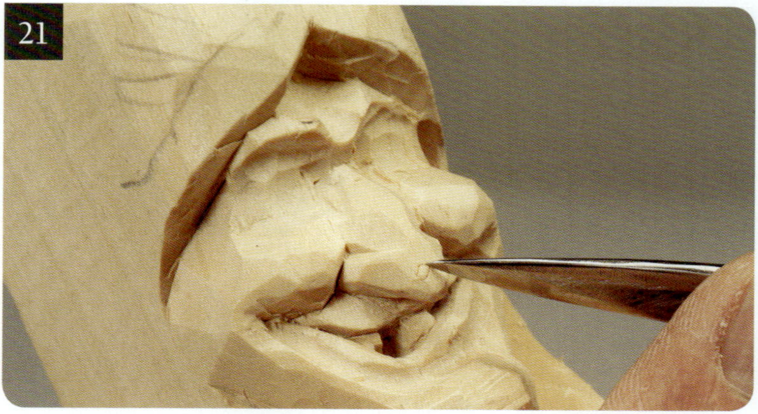

Add the wart to the nose. Stop-cut around the wart with a carving knife and relieve up to the stop cut carefully to separate the wart from the nose.

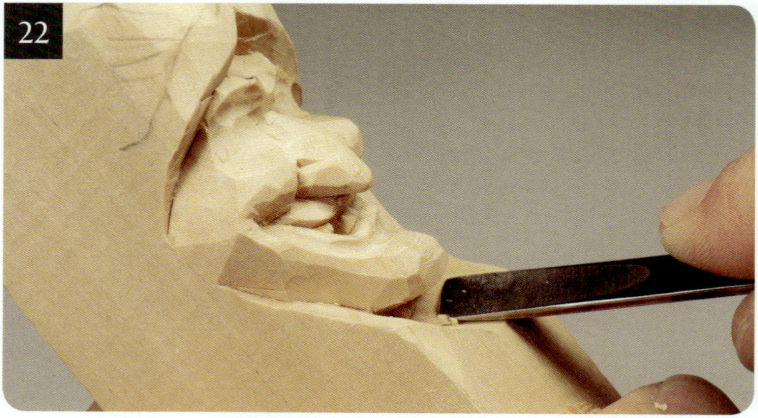

Undercut the pointed chin. Use a #3 gouge to carve under the chin so the chin sticks out from the rest of the block.

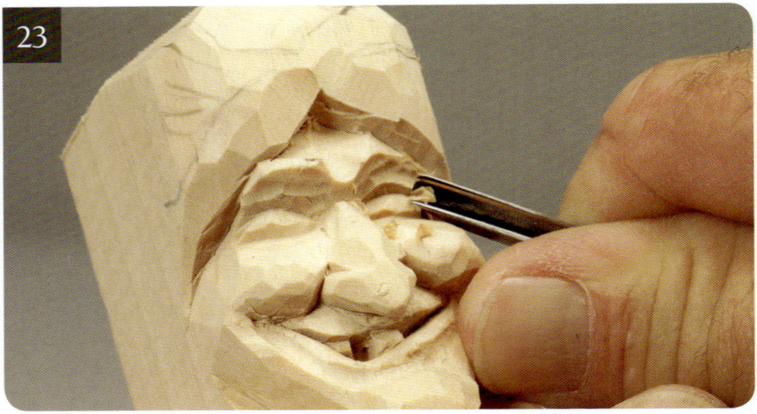

Separate the eyelids from the eye sockets. Carve along the outside edges of the eyelids with a ⅛" V-tool. This separates the eyelids from the eye sockets.

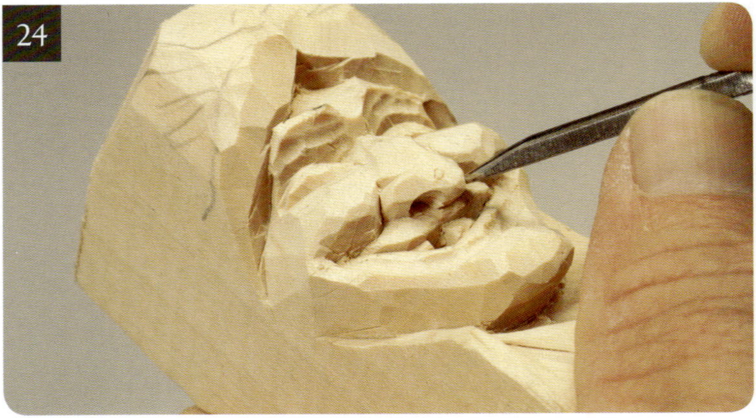

Carve the nostrils. Stab a small gouge into the nostril area. Then remove the chips with the same tool.

Carve the slitted eyes. Use a small V-tool to carefully carve along the edge of both eyelids. Carve carefully because you want only a thin slit. Use a carving knife to carefully cut up to the stop cuts and round the eyeball.

Carve the pupils. Use a micro gouge to carve a deep circle in the corners of the eyes to represent the pupils.

Carve the eyebrows. Use a ⅛" V-tool to carve a series of short grooves onto the brow line for the eyebrows.

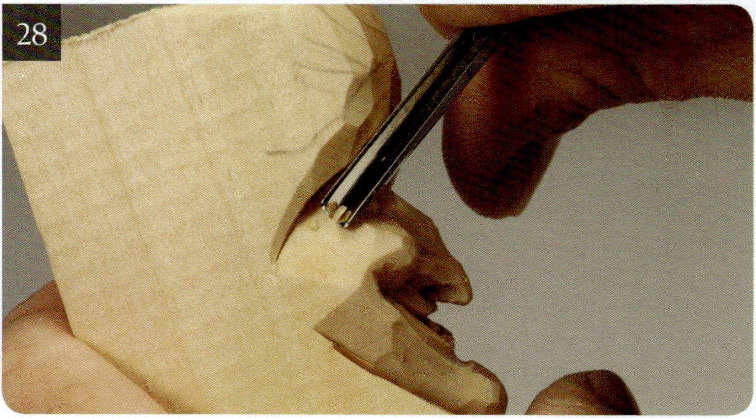

Carve the crow's feet. Use a ⅛" V-tool to add a few wrinkles and crow's feet to the corners of the eyes.

29

Shape the hair. Use a V-tool to carve the long stringy hair. Carve out from or in to the part line to emphasize the separation of the hair at the part line.

Finish carving the hair. Carve some stringy hair coming down below the chin using a small V-tool. Clean out any fuzzies with a denture brush.

More Great Study Sticks from
Harold Enlow

Carve along with Harold as he shares his carving tips and tricks with these study sticks and booklets to guide you in your carving of faces and features.

Learn to Carve Faces: Eyes and Lips
Study Stick Kit
$19.95 • Code: 5793
Booklet only
$5.99 • Code: 6226

Learn to Carve Faces: Noses and Hair
Study Stick Kit
$19.95 • Code: 5809
Booklet only
$5.99 • Code: 6233

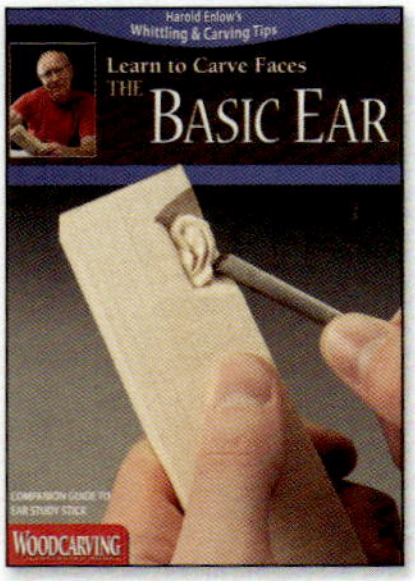

Learn to Carve Faces: The Basic Ear
Study Stick Kit
$19.95 • Code: 5816
Booklet only
$5.99 • Code: 6240

Learn to Carve Santas
Study Stick Kit
$19.95 • Code: 5786
Booklet only
$5.99 • Code: 6219

Learn to Carve Ugly Faces
Study Stick Kit
$19.95 • Code: 5830
Booklet only
$5.99 • Code: 6264

To order direct, call **800-457-9112** or visit *www.FoxChapelPublishing.com*

By mail, please send check or money order + $4.00 per book for S&H to:
Fox Chapel Publishing, 903 Square Street, Mount Joy, PA 17552